2004 POET...

# ONCE UPON
# A RHYME

## IMAGINATION FOR
## A NEW GENERATION

# London Boroughs
Edited by Chris Hallam

 Young**Writers**

First published in Great Britain in 2004 by:
Young Writers
Remus House
Coltsfoot Drive
Peterborough
PE2 9JX
Telephone: 01733 890066
Website: www.youngwriters.co.uk

SB ISBN 1 84460 595 7

# Foreword

Young Writers was established in 1991 and has been passionately devoted to the promotion of reading and writing in children and young adults ever since. The quest continues today. Young Writers remains as committed to engendering the fostering of burgeoning poetic and literary talent as ever.

This year's Young Writers competition has proven as vibrant and dynamic as ever and we are delighted to present a showcase of the best poetry from across the UK. Each poem has been carefully selected from a wealth of *Once Upon A Rhyme* entries before ultimately being published in this, our twelfth primary school poetry series.

Once again, we have been supremely impressed by the overall high quality of the entries we have received. The imagination, energy and creativity which has gone into each young writer's entry made choosing the best poems a challenging and often difficult but ultimately hugely rewarding task - the general high standard of the work submitted amply vindicating this opportunity to bring their poetry to a larger appreciative audience.

We sincerely hope you are pleased with our final selection and that you will enjoy *Once Upon A Rhyme London Boroughs* for many years to come.

# Contents

**Ravenstone Primary School**

| | |
|---|---:|
| Daniel Alaka  (9) | 66 |
| Charlotte Bedward  (8) | 67 |
| Chenai Chambers-Thomas  (9) | 68 |
| Jessica Abel  (9) | 69 |
| Nathan Watts  (9) | 70 |
| Saarah Anwar  (9) | 71 |
| Sammy Watts-Stanfield  (9) | 72 |
| Jonathan Mason  (8) | 73 |
| Laura Vitelli  (8) | 74 |

### St Joseph's Convent School, Wanstead

| | |
|---|---:|
| Claudia Zeppetella  (10) | 75 |
| Chantal Purser  (10) | 76 |
| Georgia Allpress  (10) | 77 |
| Molly Kerrigan  (10) | 78 |
| Martha Wilkinson  (10) | 79 |
| Tessa Kerslake  (9) | 80 |
| Sarah Hart  (10) | 81 |
| Jessica Lebon  (10) | 82 |
| Isabelle Carbonaro  (10) | 83 |
| Olivia Andani  (10) | 84 |
| Sophia Plent  (10) | 85 |
| Farah Omotosho  (10) | 86 |
| Georgia Feyi-Waboso  (10) | 87 |
| Harriet Blackshaw  (10) | 88 |
| Jessica Hallam  (9) | 89 |
| Clare Davis  (9) | 90 |
| Porshia Athow  (10) | 91 |
| Akua Owusu Ansah  (10) | 92 |

### St Mary Magdalene CE Primary School, Peckham

| | |
|---|---:|
| Abigail Opoku  (10) | 93 |
| Fenetta Agyemang  (11) | 94 |
| Sophie Robb  (11) | 95 |
| Shanice Smith  (11) | 96 |
| Pearl Bogle-Ivy  (11) | 97 |
| Jamel Saka  (11) | 98 |
| Fiona Ferdinand  (11) | 99 |
| Zak Carr  (10) | 100 |
| Bianca Wilson-Ebanks  (10) | 101 |
| Bimbo Akintola  (11) | 102 |

# The Poems

# What Children Need

Lots of cake
An extra large chocolate shake
Lots of sweets
Millions of treats
Pocket money going up ten pounds each day
And lots of time to play
Don't forget I don't want carrots for my tea
Fish and chips, McDonald's for me
Something else to remember
What we want, we want right now!

**Felicity King  (9)**

# London City

If you go to London City
You might see famous landmarks
Like the Natwest Tower, Big Ben
London Eye, Canary Wharf,
Houses of Parliament or The Gherkin
That looks like an Easter egg.

If you go to London City
You might see famous singers
Like 50 Cent, Ja Rule
Christina Aguilera, P Diddy
Or even the band called The Beatles.

So go to London City
You might see all these buildings
And people.

**Abdul Aziz (9)**
**Carpenters Primary School**

# Different Types Of Balls

Basketballs, footballs,
Tennis balls too.
Big balls, small balls,
Bouncy balls for you.
Hard balls, soft balls,
Rugby balls look weird.
Cricket balls, baseballs,
Sometime you won't see any near.
Bowling balls, golf balls,
Colourful balls too.
Glass balls like marbles
Wet balls and dry balls.
Silly balls, funny balls,
Happy balls and sad balls.
There are so many different types
Of balls, to choose from on the land!

**Stephanie Perucho  (9)**
**Carpenters Primary School**

# Football

Running around on the football pitch
Controlling the ball underneath my feet
Playing a team called Tiny Titch
Curling the ball to brawny Pete
Running to the wrong goal which exactly Pete's done
Scoring a goal leaving us one to none . . .
Excitement
Extraordinary
Deflated.

**Abdul Mohammed  (11)**
**Carpenters Primary School**

# Changes

C hallenges to face.
H omework to demolish.
A and getting in trouble for . . .
N o reason at all.
G reeting new teachers.
E veryone's getting along at my new . . .
S econdary school.

**Annabel Olarewaju (11)**
**Carpenters Primary School**

# Feelings

Happiness is a sprinkle of sunshine.
It is the sound of birds singing.
It is the smell of red roses.
It is the colour yellow.
It is the taste of sweet sugar.

Loneliness is the sound of the wind whistling.
It is the smell of mouldy cheese.
It is the taste of a rotten egg.
It is the feeling of being invisible.
It is the colour black.

Anger is a burst of flames.
It is the feeling of burning fire.
It is the taste of hot pepper.
It is the colour red.
It is the sound of screams.

Love is the smell of perfume.
It is the colour pink.
It is a special feeling.
It is the taste of soft lips.

**Stephanie James-Mercer (11)**
**Carpenters Primary School**

# I'm Being Bullied

They come to me with a mean face,
They trip me up when I'm doing my lace.
They take my friends and make me a loner,
Sometimes they beat me and take off one trainer.
I don't tell my teacher I'm too scared of them,
Their gang's name is 'Kill 'em'
I think about them when I go to the shop,
I wish I could hit them with a mop.
Today's the day I'm going to defeat them
With a little help from my big bro team.

**Shamima Begum  (11)**
**Carpenters Primary School**

# I Like Changes

Moving away from all your friends
It really drives me round the bend.
Moving to a different school
You know the teachers will be cruel.
Forgetting to pack your favourite shoe
Moving from the old to the new.
All the children are so rude
Teachers always in a bad mood.
Four pieces of homework and just arrived
I don't know if I can survive.

**Kayleigh Doherty (11)**
**Carpenters Primary School**

# My Life As A Baby, Infant And Child

My life as a baby was the best
Woke up, slept, and did whatever I wanted
But thing is, I hated nappy rashes.

The different things I knew as an infant
Started to know more about the world and violence,
Got scared of the dark while going down the screaming stairs
Every little noise I heard while asleep was like
The beating of a drum to signal us for the end of time.

The more I grew up
The more of a burden I had to carry
And the more things I had to do
And had to go through.
Now I have to figure myself out,
Get my life out,
Get my life straight
For the challenges ahead.

**Steeve Montanvert (11)**
**Carpenters Primary School**

# Colours And Religion

It does not matter if you're
Black or white
Asian or mixed race
It matters not in God's religion.

Nothing matters if you're different
Don't go to school
Have health problems
We're all the same in God's religion.

Just as long as you have strong faith in God
We're all the same in God's religion.

Because God loves all of us in different ways
God's love for us is big and it fits in our heart deep down.

**Elizabeth Ojo  (11)**
**Carpenters Primary School**

# You Can Be ABC

You can be . . .
An archaic archaeologist, a blue-eyed beautician,
A chivalrous chauffer, a decorative designer,
An energetic entertainer, a first-class farmer,
A gifted genius, a handy hairdresser,
An unconvinced inspector, a juvenile jogger,
A knowing king, a lanky lollipop man,
A majestic model, a nerve-racking news reporter,
An optical optician, a questioning queen,
A rich rapper, a stylish styler,
A tensed teacher, an unbeatable umpire,
A victorious violinist, a wanted waitress,
A yes man yardie, a zestful zookeeper
You can be anything you want to be
It's all out there so don't be a lazy bear!

**Ibtehal Atta-El Manan  (10)**
**Essendine Primary School**

# The You Can Be ABC

You can be . . .
An achieving artist or a bouncy ballerina
A crazy cartoonist or a devastating designer
An inventive engineer or a wittering flapping fairy
A ghetto guitarist or a hair-raising hairdresser
A jetting jogger or a knowledgeable king
A little lollipop man or a magic mechanic
A nerve-racking noisy news reporter or an outrageous operator
A popping pop star or a queer queen
A rare rapper or a swift swimmer
A terrorising tattooist or
A wicked wrestler or an excellent x-ray man
A yellow yelling yardey or a zealous zebra.

**Porscha Whittaker (10)**
**Essendine Primary School**

# The You Can Be ABC

You can be an astonishing archaeologist or a blazing bright ballerina,
A cruel crazy cartoonist or a dynamic DJ,
An enormous engineer or a fluttering fairy,
A groovy guitarist or a hairy hero,
An inquisitive inspector or a judgemental journalist,
A conniving king or a little liar,
A moody movie star or a nutty news reporter,
An open-eyed optician or a popular pop star,
A queenly queen or a rude robber,
A terrorising tattooist or an ugly umpire,
A very vicious Viking or a weird wizard
A cool X-ray man or a zany zoologist.

**Hannan Boufas (10)**
**Essendine Primary School**

# Cake

Food is the best nobody can contest
I like tea with cake
I like cake to bake
I like to be awake when my mum bakes
When we go shopping I don't like to buy tops and skirts
But I like to buy cake from the bakery
My mum thinks I should eat vegetables, cheese, milk, fruit and bread
But I prefer my cakes
Cheesecake, apple crumble, chocolate cake, fudge cake and
                                                    shortbread
Yummy for my tummy!

**Sonam Sidhu  (10)**
**Hobbayne Primary School**

# The Dolphin Song

Dolphins swim as I watch in glee
Surfing the waves almost smiling at me
Dancing and prancing before my eyes
I see the dolphins leap in surprise.

Dolphins leap through the sky
Entertaining me making me so happy I cry
No matter what people say
I'll always love dolphins in every single way!

**Shanice Sidhu  (10)**
**Hobbayne Primary School**

# Big, Big Lies

I saw a magic banana with fluffy glasses
No you never! You never! I did.
I saw a bamboo with a blue and green face
No you never! You never! I did.
I saw a dragon with painted toenails
No you never! You never! I did.
I saw a chocolate factory with lots of sprinkles
No you never! You never! I did.
I saw a colourful book with magic spells
No you never! You never! I did.
I saw a ring with magic stuff
No you never! You never! I did.
I saw a dragon with chocolate
No you never! You never! I did.
I saw a griffin with no head
No you never! You never! I did.
I saw a dragon with no foot
No you never! You never! I did.
I saw a dinosaur with spiky hair
No you never! You never! I did.
I saw a girl called Taylor with a funny nose
No you never! You never! I did.

**Kieran Monlouis  (8)**
**Holbeach Primary School**

# My Dog

I have a dog,
She is funny,
She likes a tickle on her tummy.

She is white and brown,
She is close to the ground,
But she is hard to be found.

In the morning,
She likes to play,
That's the way she starts her day.

Her ears are big,
Like a bat,
That's for hearing all the cats.

**Paige Kerr (10)**
**Ilderton Primary School**

# Rubber Me Out

I know a rubber
Full of kind,
It really has
A thoughtful mind.
Be they good
Or be they bad,
It reminds me of
The fun I had.
When children's words,
Are shouting loud,
It touches hearts
And makes me proud.
A work of heart
It is no fake,
My rubber has
A point to make.
I know a rubber, it's my friend
It always tries to help me lend,
So please do not say
Forever and today
It's wrong to love a rubber, hooray!

**Georgette Derby (10)**
**Ilderton Primary School**

# War Is Bad

W ar is not a happy life,
A ll the people are dying,
R un away before the bomb hits you.

I gnorance should stop,
S houting won't help.

B ombing should stop,
A ccidents will happen,
D ead people will never survive.

**John Choi  (9)**
**Ilderton Primary School**

# As One

We should live together
Forever and ever and ever
Never break up
And learn to make up.

We're all the same
No matter who's to blame
So let's fight together
Forever and ever.

We should stand up for our freedom rights
At the end of our nasty fights
We can live as the best
Better than the rest.

Let's stand up and fight
All day and night
Believe me it's not a pretty sight
Or should we or might.

**Chantelle Aminah-Daka (9)**
**Ilderton Primary School**

# Life And Death

We shall stand but not fall
We will win not lose
We should share not steal
We will have peace not noise
We will be good not bad.

Children's lives
During the war.
Poems dedicate
Education rises
Alive, people suffer
Crying of wars
Everyone is not alive.

**Ashley Chaise (10)**

# Book Me In

I love books now I can read
All the books I want to read
All the books in the world
All the books in the universe
All the books from everywhere
But you cannot read
All the books in the world or the universe.

**Gary Kenneth (10)**
**Ilderton Primary School**

# Our Poem

Our poem is the best
Better than the rest.
The snow is falling
The snow is calling.
The wind is calling
The snow turns to ice
It looks very nice.
We slip and fall
Then we call.
The sky is blue
The snow is white
It sticks like glue
It makes everything bright.

**Alex Ball  (9)**
**Ilderton Primary School**

# Me And My CD

I know a CD it lives with me
It's great and fun for company.
It may not look like me,
But it's a part of me.
Every CD needs a friend
That's what I'm doing till the end.
It follows me everywhere.
It jumps up and down
And turns around.

**Albert Ashdown  (10)**
**Ilderton Primary School**

# My Rabbit

I had a rabbit which jumped and bounced,
And it ran around the garden,
It ate the plants and ate the leaves,
I only wish I could keep him,
The rabbit I had was black and fluffy,
I loved him with all my heart,
I only wish I could keep him,
He had long ears and a very fluffy tail,
With fur on his head and fur on his belly,
And brown small eyes,
I only wish I could keep him
He lived in a hutch
And slept on straw,
He played in the garden
I only wish I could keep him.

**Harry Chambers  (10)**
**Ilderton Primary School**

# My Dog And Me

I have a really nice dog
I've had him since I was five
He likes to sit on a log
He's a dream boy living in a hive.

He's always there after school
He cheers me up when I'm down
He likes it when I jump in the pool
He's like a strange clown.

My dog has shaggy fur
He chases away all the cats
Although he doesn't like my friend Tur
He makes her sit on the mats.

My dog is really super
I've had him since I was five
I still have him now
Me and him are together packed in a hive.

**Shola Osho  (10)**
**Ilderton Primary School**

# Pencil In Me

I love my pencil so much.
That's a pencil no one can touch.
I just can't stop thinking about it.
I can just get a chain set
I love my pencil.
That's a pencil I love.
It reminds me of my glove.
I can use my pencil for history.
But not for biology.
I love my pencil in me.
It reminds me of the sea.

**Timi Owolabi  (10)**
**Ilderton Primary School**

# Basketball

Michael Jordan has got the ball doing slam dunks
That's why he's fit
'Cause he never eats junk.

Shaquille O'Neal has got the ball
But worst of all,
He's about to fall.

Derek Fisher has got the ball
But 'cause he's very tall
He hits his head at the top of the wall
And goes right back to the bottom
Of the floor.

**Tosin Onile  (9)**
**Ilderton Primary School**

# Teachers' Holidays

Miss Rain,
Who's very nice,
Goes to Spain,
For a very good price.

Mr Parcel,
Looking very tired,
Goes to Newcastle,
Says he's retired.

Mr Folland,
The Deputy Head,
Goes to Holland,
Looking very red.

Miss Hales,
The Head teacher,
Goes to Wales,
So no one can reach her.

Miss Drags,
Goes to Italy,
Packing her bags
Very neatly.

**Alicia Janne Widdrington-Burns (10)**
**Ilderton Primary School**

# Hidden Depths

Imagine my surprise
I had trouble breathing,
I saw my teacher on Top of the Pops that evening
Believe me I couldn't believe what I was seeing.

Her hair all red and flouncing
As she sang her hit single,
My hands began to tingle.

Her voice as I detected,
Was not as I expected,
The voice of Mrs Lawn,
Seems to have dawned.

So now my tale is told,
So remember to keep hold,
Of this page,
If you are to have a pop star for a teacher,
You could find she is a very extraordinary creature.

**Kirsten Hamilton-Allison (10)**
**Ilderton Primary School**

# Teachers' Holidays

My teacher called Mr Lance,
Flew off to visit France.
He said 'It's for the sun.'
But I bet he has lots of fun.

My head teacher would rather stay at home,
As he misses using the phone,
Sits there waiting for it to ring,
Finds he can't wait so has to sing.

Miss Baker flew off to Spain,
Even though her foot was in pain.
But she needed a break,
So she packed her cream cake.

**Chantell Broderick  (10)**
**Ilderton Primary School**

# Teachers' Holidays

Our teacher Miss Harris,
Spends her holiday in Paris,
Eats out, no grief,
But has brief with her new chief.

Our teacher Miss Price,
Goes on a plane to Spain,
Then there's Mr Test,
Who needed a holiday to have a rest.

Mrs Mason goes to Jamaica,
We can't wait to take her,
Miss Price goes to Portugal,
To watch a game of football.

There was a teacher called Miss Bent,
Who always goes away to Kent,
My teacher is Miss Berry,
Wherever she goes 'tis very merry.

**John Shadare  (10)**
**Ilderton Primary School**

# Teachers' Holidays

Tell me I am dreaming,
I can't believe my eyes,
I am stuck to the TV,
Caught in a surprise.

Tell me it's a joke,
Tell me it's not true,
Tell me it's a look-alike,
Tell me it's not Miss Prue.

I knew she could sing,
But she's going too far,
My teacher is a superstar.

I went on holiday the next day,
And what did I see,
Someone on a surfboard,
It was Mr Magee.

He was on a rollercoaster,
Soaring through the air,
I didn't want him to notice me,
So I tried not to stare.

Oh look at that monkey,
Up in that tree,
Hang on a minute,
It's our Head Miss Willoughby.

I can't wait to go to school,
When my holiday ends,
I just can't wait,
To tell my friends.

**Cheyenne Gordon  (11)**
**Ilderton Primary School**

# Secret Life Of A Teacher

Imagine my surprise,
My hair stood up on end,
Mr Baker is in disguise,
He thinks he's such a trend.

I can see him on Channel Five,
He's going mad,
It is also live,
This is so bad.

It will ruin my reputation,
He is wearing a bikini and wig,
(This is worse than my imagination)
Looking clumsy and big.

This is not so cool,
My teacher will regret it,
I don't want to go to school,
He won't forget it.

**Charley Boast (11)**
**Ilderton Primary School**

# Love

Read down and up,
And you will see,
That I found out,
That you don't love me.

If I find,
You love me still,
I'll be waiting for you,
With a meal.

Read up and down,
And you will see,
That we both love each other,
So we will be.

**Rubie-Mae Widdrington-Burns (9) & Leigh (8)**
**Ilderton Primary School**

# Dustbin Man

Every Thursday morning before you're quite awake
You hear a biff, bang, biff, bang, bash
It's the dustbin man who begins with a biff, bang, biff, bang, bash.

You hop out of bed
And you appear with a rash, and crash down the stairs.
Then I dash out of the door and complain.

When I went outside I said 'You'll be dead
If you don't let me go to my bed.'

**Rosie Ajuna  (9)**
**Ilderton Primary School**

# When Gran Went To The Moon

When Gran went to the moon
She had tea on the moon
She came back at noon and played a happy tune
She asked herself 'What should I do?
I can go to the market with my big brown basket
Or stay at home and hum my happy tune
Or my granddaughter Lydia can stay with me all afternoon.'

**Amber Loffler (8)**
**Ilderton Primary School**

# When Gran Went To The Moon

When Mum went to the moon
She said 'I will come back soon!'
When Gran went to the moon
She found a wooden spoon.

**Daniella Connor  (8)**
**Ilderton Primary School**

# When Dad Went To The Moon

When Dad went to the Moon
It was noon
Then he saw a room
He went in the room to get a spoon
And ended up locked in a tomb
And Dad lay in the tomb.

**Henry Arko-Dadzie  (8)**
**Ilderton Primary School**

# Clare McFlare

Clare McFlare had beautiful hair
Clare McFlare sat on a chair
She went outside and had a ride
On a friendly big, brown, bear

The friendly big, brown, bear
Was calling Clare McFlare
For a walk and a talk
And they both played truth or dare.

**Elizabeth Su  (8)**
**Ilderton Primary School**

# The Cat

The cat sat on a rat
It was sitting on the floor
Then the cat took off his hat
And replaced it on the door.

The cat eats jelly
Hold my coat
Watch my belly
I felt like I'm about to float.

I felt very sick
So I ate some jelly
Then I picked some sticks
And watched some telly.

**Ruchelle Broderick  (8)**
**Ilderton Primary School**

# When Dad Went To The Moon

When Dad went to the Moon
It was noon
When he saw a balloon
Inside the balloon was a room
He popped the balloon
And went into the room
And flew out on a big old broom.

**Ciaran McDonnell (7)**
**Ilderton Primary School**

# Football

Football is cool,
It's the best of all,
I wish that Thierry Henry
Came to our school
Well, that's all.

Football is like a duel,
The team goes cruel,
Like the whole pitch goes tall
That's why Reyes is cool.

Football is cool,
The pitch goes like a pool
That's why Ronaldo goes
Like a fool.

**Eric Ekanem (9)**
**Ilderton Primary School**

# The Cat

The cat had a hat
It had a suit
It did a rap
And it had a boot.

In my garden I saw a cat
It did a burp
Its name was Pat
It went down the kerb.

I had a cat
I brought it to school
My mate had a hat
Then we jumped in a pool.

I had a cat
I took it home
It lay on the mat
And my mum got the comb.

**Charlie Ward  (9)**
**Ilderton Primary School**

# Love Letter

Alison is crying
Roger starts trying
Roger breaks her heart
She starts crying to Bart.
So Alison is cross
And feels like moss.
She tries to make a laugh
But they go to have a bath.
Roger is a grass
Just like brass.

So she wrote a letter to Peter
Saying 'Dear Peter I love you.'
He wrote a letter back saying
'I love you too.'
So Roger was impressed
Alison stopped being a pest.
Peter was annoyed that she needs to rest.

**Sarah Pocock  (9)**
**Ilderton Primary School**

# Shop Till You Drop!

Today I'm not going to school,
I think that I'm going to shop
Everybody thinks that I'm cool,
I'm going to spend until I drop.

I think I'm going to shop
I might go and buy me some shoes
I'm going to spend until I drop
I know I will gain what I lose.

I might go and buy me some shoes
The teacher appeared over there
I know I will gain what I lose
Then I said to myself, 'Beware!'

The teacher appeared over there
Then she sent me to class
Then I said to myself, 'Beware!'
Then I got a detention at last.

Then she sent me to class
Everybody thinks I'm cool
Then I got a detention at last
Today I'm not going to school.

**Rebecca Raper (10)**
**Ilderton Primary School**

# My Grandma

My grandma loves to eat
With her dirty feet
She farts in her seat
And loves to eat sweets.

She never brushes her teeth
And has a boyfriend named Keith
He's a big fat thief
And loves to eat wheat.

My grandma really hates me
She will never let me be
That's why I never see her
And that's all about my grandma!

**Jadesola Gbadebo (10)**
**Ilderton Primary School**

# Absent!

Today I'm not going to school,
I pretended I'm very sick.
Everyone thinks I'm a fool,
But skiving gives me a real kick.

I pretended I'm very sick,
I painted some spots on my face,
But skiving gives me a real kick,
The nurse say's I've got a bad case.

I painted some spots on my face,
I know that I'm being very bad.
The nurse says I've got a bad case,
But I'm happy instead of being sad.

I know that I'm being very bad,
All day I'll be watching TV,
And I'm happy instead of being sad,
Watching rubbish fills me with glee.

All day I'll be watching TV,
Everyone thinks I'm a fool.
Watching rubbish fills me with glee,
Today I'm not going to school!

**Ogechi Amadi  (10)**
**Ilderton Primary School**

# My Grandad

My grandad likes to bend,
To try and pretend,
To cuddle and kiss me,
To try and see,
If I want multicoloured milk for tea.

His beard says,
To be good always,
And his nails scratches,
Like a box of matches,
That my cat always catches.

**Tunde Adeniyi (10)**
**Ilderton Primary School**

# Rumours All Rumours

She was spreading rumours all over the school,
And told everyone I was cool.

She threw all my things away
Then she said to me, 'Go away.'

Sharon always cries
And she's always bad
She told my sister a pack of lies
And went home sad.

She ripped my blouse
And cut my scarf
Threw eggs at my house
Tore my T-shirt in half.

**Gary Wells  (10)**
**Ilderton Primary School**

# Here Comes A Wizard

Here comes a wizard,
He's not casting a spell,
He's riding his mad motorbike,
On the way to Hell.
He needs to meet the devil,
To get a red-hot pebble,
'Cos, he's feeling very ill,
That's why the pebble is a pill,
Now the poem has gladly ended,
He is well and goodly mended,
His only task now,
Is to milk his ugly cow.

**Joab Evans Campbell  (10)**
**Ilderton Primary School**

# I'm In Dreamland

I'm in Dreamland,
It is so hot,
There is lots of sand,
In the small pot.

Dreamland is the best.
That's what you can't test.
It is so nice
Without any mice.

Come to Dreamland
And you will see,
Should I tell you what you will see?
You will see me.

**Duncan Hamilton-Allison (8)**
**Ilderton Primary School**

# There Was A Dog

There was a dog called Sam
That had a funny nan
He had a cousin called Pam
Who lived with a man.

There was a lady called Donny
Who had a baby called Sonny
She had a dog Sam
Who knew his cousin Pam.

**Fatima Turay  (8)**
**Ilderton Primary School**

# The Farmer!

There was a farmer who had some sheep,
And everyday he'd shave them clean,
He'll take his tractor, carry them around,
And end up in a baby crowd.

**Helen Spincemaille (9)**
**Ilderton Primary School**

# Kenny

There was a girl called Kenny
Who nicked a big, round penny.
Then got put into jail
And then she began to wail.

**Lauren Lynch  (9)**
**Ilderton Primary School**

# My Tiger

I have a tiger,
She drinks lager,
Then she eats lava,
She burps and farts
And flames come out.

She carries me to bed,
She makes me tea,
She goes to bed,
That means she's dead.

I buried her in the ground,
But she's loud under the ground,
Now she's a ghost,
She really boasts.

**Carl Townsend  (9)**
**Ilderton Primary School**

# My Teacher

My teacher once was a baby
My teacher used to cry
My teacher once wore nappies
My teacher said goodbye.

My teacher is all grown-up now
My teacher is so cool
My teacher thinks she's different
My teacher is not at all.

**Michelle Duong  (10)**
**Ilderton Primary School**

# Miss G Host

We're sitting in class throwing paper planes,
When the supply teacher comes in,
She's ghostly white and very pale,
And she said 'What a din!'
She looked at us with dark black eyes,
A scowl on her ugly face,
It was clear she doesn't like,
The children of the human race.
Then she says 'Class I must go out'
And out she does go,
Then she locks the door and pulls the fire alarm,
And laughs from the other side of the window.
Then she walks through the locked door
And said in a chilling voice
'Come down to Hell for a little snack'
And as we went down she disappeared and began to rejoice
For you see Miss G Host
Is really a ghost!

**Hayley Osborne (11)**
**Ilderton Primary School**

# A Beautiful Poem

Lift to your ear the gleaming wave-washed shell
Its song may tell ancient sea life tales
Of the thought of people calling me in the water
The sound of the waves touching the sand
The treasure chest wide open waiting to be found
The sun shining all its light on me
The feel of myself falling deep into the sea
The echo of the dolphins playing and jumping in the air.

**Rhiana Green  (8)**
**Ravenstone Primary School**

# The Wondrous Sea

Lift to your ears
The gleaming wave-washed shell
Its songs may tell
Ancient sea life tales
Of water lords ruling underwater cities.
Rusty ships once sailed the seven seas
Now remain
Redundant
Dead
Broken.
A place for fish
With sailors' memories
Then there are worlds
Made out of coral
Fish, seaweed and rocks
But be careful
Some fish might
Not welcome you
Corals disguised a jellyfish
Doing a handstand
A school of fish on
A school journey
Swim into a pool of light.

**Miles Bassett (9)**
**Ravenstone Primary School**

# Sea Life Poem

Lift to your ear
The gleaming wave-washed shell
Its song may tell
Ancient sea life tales
Of mermaids singing softly at sea
An arched shape of diving dolphins
Leap at sea
The forbidden scattered treasure
The outline of a sunken ship
At the bottom of sea
The peaceful underwater place
Seals waddling to shore
Sharks coming to attack
Musty broken anchors
Lost in the sea.

**Rebecca Jones  (9)**
**Ravenstone Primary School**

# Seashell Two

Lift to your ear
The gleaming wave-washed shell
Its song may tell
Ancient sea life tales
Of flapping fins of fish gently swishing their tails
Of skeletons of wrecked ships peacefully floating away
Diving dolphins making mystical arch-like shapes
And tales of dazzling treasure chests unsecured underwater
Legends of mermaids combing their golden hair and
Poseidon sitting on his throne
Peacefully resting away leaning on his trident.

**Alexander Clark  (8)**
**Ravenstone Primary School**

# The Seashell

Lift to your ear
The gleaming wave-washed shell
Its song may tell
Ancient sea life tales of
Small shells sailing in the sea
And crabs clicking their claws
Fish flapping their tails
The silent sounds in the sea
Mermaids brushing their long curly hair
Shiny shells in the sea.

**Aaliyah Wright (9)**
**Ravenstone Primary School**

# Sea Tales

Lift to your ear
The gleaming wave-washed shell
Its song may tell
Ancient sea life tales
Of fish zooming across
The seabed floor.
Of swordfish slicing like
Swords attacking their prey.
Of eels hiding in the dark,
Waiting for prey.
Of gold pieces spilling
Out of the chest
Of dolphins leaping over the sea
Of Neptune on his throne
With his trident
Of clams snapping like crocodiles.

**Rhys Harford  (9)**
**Ravenstone Primary School**

# The Sea

Lift to your ear
The gleaming wave-washed shell
Its song may tell
Ancient sea life tales
Of a peaceful palace
And lovely landscapes
Of crabs clicking claws
Click, click
The shoals and shoals of fish
And perching pearls in opened oysters
The walls of weed
Tales of washing waves
And the arched shape of diving dolphins
That's the tale it may tell.

**Saskia Menti  (9)**
**Ravenstone Primary School**

# The Ocean

Lift to your ear
The gleaming wave-washed shell
Its song may tell
Ancient sea life tales
Of all over the sea
The sea is like a big dog
The flapping of fins of fish
The swordfish dangers, a shoal of fish
Big whales swallowing fish
The teeth of the shark
And like knives
Dolphins diving in and out of the water.

**Daniel Alaka  (9)**
**Ravenstone Primary School**

# A Seashell Tale

Lift to your ear
The gleaming wave-washed shell
Its song may tell
Ancient sea life tales
Of seaweed swishing softly
And fish swimming along gently
Of dolphins diving in and out
And crabs walking side to side
The giant beams of light
Showing flapping fins of little fish
The peaceful water hides glinting gold
An old boat invaded with sharks
It would be a shame to sell
The old seashell.

**Charlotte Bedward (8)**
**Ravenstone Primary School**

# Shell Of Life

Lift to your ear
The gleaming wave-washed shell
Its song may tell
Ancient sea life tales
Of a sweet song
Of misty mermaids
Beckoning sailors to the shore.
The dim light
Of the dim and dusty
Colourful fish swim with a rush
The shoal of fish live the life of a shell
A shell of life.

**Chenai Chambers-Thomas  (9)**
**Ravenstone Primary School**

# Seashell

Lift to your ear
The gleaming wave-washed shell
Its song may tell
Ancient sea life tales
Of mermaids, their souls lost to the sea
And a swish of a clown fish's tail
White with curiosity
My mind swimming to the caves filled with nature
Of sailors who lost their lives, moaning
And the musty smell of sunken ships
A swing of a shark's tail
A splash of a dolphin's fin
The everlasting call of Neptune
A glimpse of a fish tale lurking, lurking over there.

**Jessica Abel  (9)**
**Ravenstone Primary School**

# Underwater Ocean

Lift to your ear
The gleaming wave-washed shell
Its song may tell
Ancient sea life tales
Of the fishes swimming deep, deep down
In the ocean
Of the bottom of the back of a submarine
And dangerous creatures approaching their prey
Of fishes looking at beautiful colours
And sharks doing their 3 on 1 on the clown fish
Of crabs scraping the bottom of the ocean
With their sharp claws and feet
Of rusty bites
Of whelks scraping along the floor
Of the bottom of the ocean shining
By golden treasure glowing bright and lovely.

**Nathan Watts  (9)**
**Ravenstone Primary School**

# The Sea World

Lift your ear
The gleaming wave-washed shell
Its song may tell
Ancient sea life tales
Of the wind blowing waves
And galloping dolphins
And fishes flapping fins and wiggling their tails side to side
With ships sinking deeper and deeper
As the sinking ship drowns, the rotten smell spreads
With the scattering smell of bones at the bottom of the sea.

**Saarah Anwar  (9)**
**Ravenstone Primary School**

# In The Ocean

Lift to your ear
The gleaming wave-washed shell
Its song may tell
Ancient sea life tales
Of ancient gleaming gold
The sound of waves hitting the water while breaking
And if you're a fish you'll see old underwater caves
God's making powers up in the sky and making storms
With old rusty anchors stuck in the sand
And attached to them are half broken shipwrecks
Ancient gleaming gold with old bones all around it.

**Sammy Watts-Stanfield  (9)**
**Ravenstone Primary School**

# The Sea

Lift to your ear
The gleaming wave-washed shell
Its song may tell
Ancient sea life
Tales of Neptune on his throne
Rusty anchors beneath coral
Broken ships without life
Sharks' teeth going through prey like knives.

**Jonathan Mason (8)**
**Ravenstone Primary School**

# Water World

Lift to your ear
The gleaming wave-washed shell
Its song may tell
Ancient sea life tales
Of silver mermaids,
And sirens' songs, echoing through the ocean,
Like so many church singers in unison
Of rainbowfish darting hither and thither,
And the mournful call of Neptune on his coral throne
Of frothing waves crashing onto the sand, or parting in shallow water
Of giant clams catching only plankton in vain.

**Laura Vitelli (8)**
**Ravenstone Primary School**

# Midnight Express

Chucka! Chucka! Chucka! Through the green deep meadows
Roaring, cheering, banging, raging as if a war waging
Is it a cheetah or a fifty-legged spider?
Pink and purple mounts, high up in the sky.
Steam that makes you dream
Of candy canes and cookies, drifting through the steam.
Not a worry in the world only the midnight breaking.
Owls tweeting and children sleeping
As hushaby row, goes rolling by
Only two hoots fill the roofs of the children sleeping
Whoo, whoo!

**Claudia Zeppetella (10)**
**St Joseph's Convent School, Wanstead**

# The Lightning Express

Rushing and rushing against the wind,
Like a lot of bullets being fired
Goes the express train.
Sheep are eating,
Workers are meeting.
Everything was fine that day.
Sheep are bleating,
Cows are sleeping,
The train is almost halfway there.
The day is oh so sunny.
Blurry people look so funny!
Everything was fine that day.
The Lightning Express
Is now slowing down
It comes to a halt
And chug! Chug! Chug!

**Chantal Purser (10)**
**St Joseph's Convent School, Wanstead**

# How It Feels To Be A Fish

As I swim into the deep, dark sea
The deeper you go the darker it will be.

Lots of fishes big and small
It's so much fun to see them all.

So many colours beautiful and bright,
I am so excited and filled with delight.

All of a sudden a dolphin flashed past me to say 'Hello'
And then I realised it was time to go.

**Georgia Allpress (10)**
**St Joseph's Convent School, Wanstead**

# On The Way To San Francisco

Riding through a field,
I kept my eyes peeled,
For the owl I could hear,
Hooting down my ear.
I passed some trees,
Blown by the train's breeze
The leaves are on the ground,
Spinning, round and round.

**Molly Kerrigan  (10)**
**St Joseph's Convent School, Wanstead**

# Secrets Of The Deep

As I plunged down bubbles surround me,
Like pearls around me.
Sliding down the deep,
To the surface of the sea.
Like an intruder, on and on I sink.
As I slither through the ocean world.
Dominated by fishes of all types,
Sparkling like multicoloured diamonds.
But it is too cold, as cold as the Antarctic.
The clasping, gripping, freezing cold.
Pulling me to the surface, holding me,
Pulling me, gripping me back to the ordinary world.

**Martha Wilkinson  (10)**
**St Joseph's Convent School, Wanstead**

# Under The Surface

Under the surface, down I go,
Down I creep.
As I search the deep a fish comes to my feet
Under the surface
I feel like an intruder
Cold crawls over me like a tarantula
I flip my flippers to and fro
And back up I swim.

**Tessa Kerslake  (9)**
**St Joseph's Convent School, Wanstead**

# The Train To Glasgow

The train was beeping,
The sheep was leaping,
The black train,
The track lane,
The day is nice, so
The mice play.

The day was funny,
A bunny was sunny,
The train was fast,
The train was at last there;
Not a flutter,
Just a clutter,
Arriving in Glasgow.

**Sarah Hart  (10)**
**St Joseph's Convent School, Wanstead**

# Wales Express

Such a sunny day,
Puffing smoke every minute.
As fast as a cheetah!
As scary as lightning!
Sometimes even very frightening!
Making such a big wind.
As she travels through the countryside.
So many noises as she goes along.
Choo, whoo, chuff, roar!
A lot of views of the lovely hills, meadows and animals,
So many beautiful and different varieties of flowers.
High up in the sky you can see an air balloon.
Big and green, rattling along, the express,
But soon getting slower and calmer as she reaches Wales.

**Jessica Lebon (10)**
**St Joseph's Convent School, Wanstead**

# The Lightning Train

Like a shooting star, the lightning train chuffs by.
Whistles like a kettle
Glitters like a string of bullets,
Its hold is a clutter of mail
Like a knife through butter.
Clean wheels,
Grey motion,
Travelling in fast luxury
Through golden meadows
Letters blowing all the way
To La Yole.
At the least get us to France
Safely while it lasts.

**Isabelle Carbonaro  (10)**
**St Joseph's Convent School, Wanstead**

# Plunging Through The Deep Beyond

As I swim through the sea beyond
All I can see is the blackness of coal
I feel like an intruder
Stealing away their home
As fishes swim beneath me
I can feel a tingle in my toes
I hear a whisper
Then my mind goes wild
Could this be sea creatures whispering in liquid silence?
Whispering by my feet
Could this, would this be true?
I shall never know
For my leg has gone lame
I must come up and end my journey
But as I swim up
I see seaweed sway side by side to the rhythm of the tide
As if to say goodbye.

**Olivia Andani  (10)**
**St Joseph's Convent School, Wanstead**

# The Night Mail Train

Whizzing round in the dark of night,
I have to get there before light,
I'm clean and sleek,
I'm around when you're asleep.
I am a fast, silent, jet-black train,
Even faster than a plane,
Flashing past the lush green grass,
Even through the sticky marsh,
In the fields horses, cows and sheep,
Don't hear me when they're asleep.

**Sophia Plent  (10)**
**St Joseph's Convent School, Wanstead**

# My Discos

My discos are so loud and proud, when we're
Dancing and prancing and singing and signing,
Opening and wrapping and kissing and hugging,
Eating and drinking and pushing and shoving,
Gossiping and aahing and giving and taking,
Asking and telling and jumping and bumping,
Laughing and tasting and showing off and going off,
Comparing and tearing and competing and cheating!

Cheering and jeering and playing and saying,
Hopping and stopping and staying and paying,
Moaning and groaning and bobbing and popping,
Running and skipping and starting and larking,
Flashing and dashing and walking and talking,
Spying and tying and making up and breaking up,
Cutting and sticking and whirling and turning,
Ticking and picking and pinging and clinging!

Yelling and smelling and sipping and dipping,
Annoying and enjoying and licking and flinging,
Chiming and timing and banging and clanging,
Writing and lighting and blowing and glowing,
Looking and booking and bashing and clashing!
Oh such a lovely atmosphere.

**Farah Omotosho (10)**
**St Joseph's Convent School, Wanstead**

# Here Comes The Cardiff Train

Past the wet greenery,
Through the countryside,
Big tall green scenery,
Where the fox and her cubs hide,
Her purring sound going past,
Fiercely rushing, rushing very fast.

Anxious people waiting for post,
Waiting for post they want the most,
The screeching sound as it brakes,
The milkman shouting as he wakes.

The smooth ride, music to my ears;
No worries, no cares, no little fears!
Just when it starts to rain, here comes the Cardiff train!

**Georgia Feyi-Waboso (10)**
**St Joseph's Convent School, Wanstead**

# Hollywood Express

Chuffing fast, passing green grass,
Plumes of smoke like dolphins leaping out!

Riding on the tracks,
Sending special packs.

Riding round the bend,
This will never, ever end!

Riding fast,
Never going to be last!

Always going to win,
Let's go for a spin!

**Harriet Blackshaw  (10)**
**St Joseph's Convent School, Wanstead**

# The Horse Wood Express

The train quickly rushes by
And people put all their letters in to go to Dubai.
Chucka, chucka, chucka comes the train,
Down the tracks of the quiet lane.
Hurrying down the tracks like starlight,
Horses, cows, pigs and sunlight.
The Horse Wood Train runs through the countryside,
People stare as it goes by.
It stops at the station, slowing down.
Wheels will stop there,
People come rushing as it approaches the station.
Off it starts running again,
Flowers, all different kinds, blow as it runs by.
On it goes to the next nearest station.
Finally it arrives at Dubai
And says to the letters and people, 'Goodbye!'

**Jessica Hallam  (9)**
**St Joseph's Convent School, Wanstead**

# Midnight Express

The powerful dark green Midnight Express!
Whizzing past green bushes and trees.
Creaky, rattling, squeaky wheels,
Going mile after mile, day after day.
Hours quickly going, days shooting past.

The powerful wind howling at night,
Terrifying passers by.
Midnight Express flying past rolling hills
Clattering, rattling by passing fields,
Lights beaming in the darkness of night,
Until the light of day.

Whizzing down the track,
Stretching out as if it is on the rack.
Never stopping, always moving, it's . . .
The Midnight Express.

**Clare Davis  (9)**
**St Joseph's Convent School, Wanstead**

# Himalayas Express

Dashing through the mountains,
The whistles mighty bellow,
Isolated from the world,
The Himalayas Express.
Velvet-red and holly-green,
Out of the funnel comes steam, steam, steam.
From the planes high in the sky,
It looks like a string of beads whizzing by.
The Himalayas Express is clattering high,
High in the mountains against the sky.
To the Himalayas Express we bid goodbye,
For we've run out of coal.
Oh my! Oh my!

**Porshia Athow  (10)**
**St Joseph's Convent School, Wanstead**

# Stormy Sea

The sea is strong and gushes along
Clashing, thrashing, splashing and crashing,
Bashing and dashing, whirring and twirling,
Furling and curling side to side in the fierce tide.
Rising and leaping, sinking and creeping,
Hitting and splitting, moaning and groaning
Pouring and roaring, slapping and rapping
And clapping and tapping,
Bumping, thumping, jumping and pumping along.

**Akua Owusu Ansah  (10)**
**St Joseph's Convent School, Wanstead**

# What Are They Saying?

I thought they were my friends
But now they leave me out
They're whispering now, what's it all about?
Those three are always talking,
They're pointing at me too.
I ask someone what they're saying
She says they are 'Talking about you!'

**Abigail Opoku  (10)**
**St Mary Magdalene CE Primary School, Peckham**

# Be Quiet!

'Be quiet,' my sister whispered hitting me on the hand,
'Be quiet and listen to the steel band.'
I feel the breeze rushing down my neck,
I stop and wait just for a sec.
I hear lots of little voices,
Making very loud noises.
I am sitting here fiddling with my hair.
Everyone's coming out of the church,
Acting like I'm not there.

**Fenetta Agyemang  (11)**
**St Mary Magdalene CE Primary School, Peckham**

# A Whisper Is Like . . .

A whisper is like the ocean,
Like footsteps creeping up and downstairs.
Like a wind blowing,
Like a baby breathing.

Sometimes I whisper to my friends
When I'm telling one of my secrets.

**Sophie Robb  (11)**
**St Mary Magdalene CE Primary School, Peckham**

# Whisper

As I was in my bed I could hear
Whispers from a far distance.
Whoosh . . . whoosh . . . whoosh . . .
It sounded like the ocean,
Like a whale in the bathroom.

Whoosh . . . whoosh . . . whoosh . . . but this time
The noise sounded different
Like a fish breathing out of its gills,
Like hearing mermaids singing their songs to each other.

**Shanice Smith  (11)**
**St Mary Magdalene CE Primary School, Peckham**

# Shut Up Or I Will . . .

'Shut up or I will . . .
Shout at you
Storm out of the room
Or hit you with a broom.

Shut up or I will . . .
Tear up all your stuff
Slap you in the face you big disgrace

Shut up or I will
Shout, shout, shout
Will you just shut up!'

**Pearl Bogle-Ivy (11)**
**St Mary Magdalene CE Primary School, Peckham**

# Dark Whispers

I hear whispers in the night
I hear whispers that give me a fright.
They travel here in the air,
And escape secretly through my ear.
I am in my bed scared and alone,
With the lights turned off and not one on.
I am all alone, no one here beside me,
All my family's gone.
I am afraid, very . . . afraid.

**Jamel Saka (11)**
**St Mary Magdalene CE Primary School, Peckham**

# Shouting Is Like

Shouting is me singing out loud.
It sometimes makes me proud.
Shouting is when my parents tell me to go to bed,
I watch TV all night instead.

**Fiona Ferdinand  (11)**
**St Mary Magdalene CE Primary School, Peckham**

# Underwater Whisper

Underwater whisper
The bubbles, the silent bubbles
I hear the waves swishing
Deep down I hear dolphins calling out, singing
Whales coming to the surface
The water running off its back
The soft echo is beautiful, it's the quiet whisper
That's the sound of underwater whisper.

**Zak Carr (10)**
**St Mary Magdalene CE Primary School, Peckham**

# Brother And Sisters

'I hate you!'
'I hate you too!'

'You smell like wee!'
'You smell like poo!'

'Look at you, you stupid elf!'
'Look at you with your ugly self!'

'You think you're smart!'
'You think you're cool!'

'You're really ugly!'
'You look like a mule!'

'You have a very ugly face!'
'Look at you, you're a disgrace!'

'You shouldn't be in this human race!'
'You can't even tie your own shoelace!'

'You two stop having a row,
Forget about it and make up now.'

'I love you'
'I love you too'

'You still smell like wee!'
'You still smell like poo!'

**Bianca Wilson-Ebanks (10)**
**St Mary Magdalene CE Primary School, Peckham**

# Whispers

He was whispering
She was whispering
Shhhh
They were whispering
Everyone was whispering
I wonder what they were saying?

**Bimbo Akintola  (11)**
**St Mary Magdalene CE Primary School, Peckham**

# Whoosh

Have you put your ear on a seashell?
And it makes a loud whoosh
Isn't it such a beautiful sound?

**Thomas Elliott  (11)**
**St Mary Magdalene CE Primary School, Peckham**

# Whispers

A whisper is . . .

Like a grasshopper
Tickling my fingers,

The settling down of a tiger wave
Coming in gently,

Men and women going ice-skating
And spinning,

Like two people making a wish
Of love.

**Amoiya Barnett-Wallen  (8)**
**St Mary Magdalene CE Primary School, Peckham**

# The Fall Of Spain

Guns to the left,
Guns to the right,
The battle is starting to become tight.

The Spanish began to attack
Sending the Turks back,
Alas this was not great
They became sitting bait.

The guns roared into the air,
Sounding like water beginning to tear.

When the men heard this,
They began to hiss.

Spanish tried one last attack
But were sent all the way back.

As the mists vanished
And the smells banished,
There lay the Spanish on the floor
Realising they were no more.

**Felix Coid  (11)**
**St Paul's Cathedral School, London**

# Death

I've got a meeting with Death,
At the other end of the trenches.

I've started my long journey,
Through the Valley of Death.

Suddenly I look up,
And see a plane exploding.

I fall over a half
Rotted away body.

I stagger onwards through
Puddles of blood.

On the shore I see
A jerry ship sinking.

I know these brave men
Will die a heroes death.

Finally I reach the
End of the trenches.

Death isn't here,
I must be early.

I recall all the horrors,
Of my long journey.

I've been waiting for months,
While I rot away.

Waiting for Death,
To come and claim me.

Suddenly it hits me,
I must be Death.

All the horrors I've seen,
I have caused them.

I am the killer,
Of all creation!

**Peter Dennison  (11)**
**St Paul's Cathedral School, London**

# The Sea Shanty Of The Pirates

On the desert island,
Where the caveman stands.

There is a purple mountain,
With a little green goat.

On the desert island,
Where the caveman stands.

There is a small red river,
With a big fat pike.

On the desert island,
Where the caveman stands.

There is a huge black forest,
With a multicoloured parrot.

This is what I see,
As I am sailing past.

I've got a ship full of treasure,
And a crew with no teeth.

**Arthur Fuest  (11)**
**St Paul's Cathedral School, London**

# What Could You Do On A Rainy Day?

Mary Dotion,
Mary Dotion,
One day she had an amazing notion!
Amazing notion,
Amazing notion,
Was to make an evil, evil potion!
Evil potion,
Evil potion,
Made from shampoo and body lotion!
Body lotion,
Body lotion,
Could be poisonous in an evil potion.
Poisonous potion,
Poisonous potion,
Made by crafty Mary Dotion,
Mary Dotion,
Mary Dotion,
Made it because of her awful emotions,
Awful emotions,
Awful emotions,
About horrible Grandma Dotion,
Grandma Dotion,
Grandma Dotion,
Drank the horrible, horrible potion.
Horrible potion,
Horrible potion,
Killed poor and horrible Grandma Dotion.
Grandma Dotion,
Grandma Dotion,
Killed by shampoo and body lotion!

**Matthew Hilborn  (11)**
**St Paul's Cathedral School, London**

*Young Writers - Once Upon A Rhyme London Boroughs*

# The Merry Mishaps Of Arthur Fuest

Arthur Fuest
Arthur Fuest
Stuck his foot in a pigeon roost

Pigeon roost
Pigeon roost
Hung on tight to Arthur Fuest

Arthur Fuest
Arthur Fuest
Hanging from the pigeon roost

Pigeon roost
Pigeon roost
Did not at all like Arthur Fuest

Arthur Fuest
Arthur Fuest
Saw a farmer and made a truce

Made a truce
Made a truce
The farmer truced with Arthur Fuest

Arthur Fuest
Arthur Fuest
Finally down from the pigeon roost

Pigeon roost
Pigeon roost
Was devoid of Arthur Fuest

Arthur Fuest
Arthur Fuest
Went back home and ate some mousse.

Moral

Pigeon roosts,
Do not like Fuests
And neither do most moose.

**Cem Hurrell (11)**
**St Paul's Cathedral School, London**

# Trouble In Toon Town

Little Red Riding Hood she found a shoe!
A beautiful, gleaming, high-heeled shoe,
The problem was it was covered in honey,
So she decided to sell it for a little money.

You'll never guess who bought the shoe
It was none other than Winnie the Pooh!
She sold it for only two pence
But for Winnie, this was a great expense.

On the way home he bumped into Mickey
Who told Pooh 'Your shoe is awfully sticky!'
Pooh replied, 'You stupid mouse!
This is an ornament, of course for my house!'

Mickey exclaimed, 'So the sticky stuff's glue?'
'No, it's honey!' said Winnie the Pooh.
On the way home, Pooh took a bite
When along came an officer who started a fight!

'How dare you!' he screamed, 'You stupid fool!
You are eating Cinderella's shoe!'
'Listen,' he replied, 'the name is Winnie.'
But after all exchanged it for Cinder's Pinny.

**Safiah Ngah  (11)**
**St Paul's Cathedral School, London**

# A Death In The Savannah

Slowly crawling and creeping,
Waiting in the rustling grass for his prey,
While the sun is setting somewhere far away,
Waiting carefully, he lay.
He lay.
A pack of gazelles,
A flock of scavenger birds,
A sunset slowly disappearing,
Picture the scene where he lay.
He lay.
Suddenly, he sprang,
In a moment of beauty and grace,
He flew through the air,
And pounced on his prey.
His prey.
A chase was drawn up,
No words could describe it,
Moments of might and of fear,
As he gracefully danced with his prey.
His prey.

**Alex Nikolov  (11)**
**St Paul's Cathedral School, London**

# Myself

I am the sun beaming in the sky,
I am a magnificent bird swooping high.

I am this poem, the rhythm and the rhyme,
I am the tick-tock of a clock that tells the time.

I am the present in which gives you so much joy,
I am the comfort of a soft and snugly toy.

I am the animal roaming free and wild,
I am the fun and youth of a happy child.

I am everything that I possibly could be,
But if you add these things together then you'll find just truly me!

**Ruby Radley  (10)**
**St Paul's Cathedral School, London**

# The Mummified Pharaoh

There was once a mummy,
Who was tired of sleeping in his pharaoh box tummy,
As he spat out his bandaged up dummy,
He smelt something rather yummy,
He came across something rather funny,
Which looked a bit like honey,
But it was far too runny,
So he decided to go back to sleep,
In his sarcophagus tummy.

**Timothy Sapsford (11)**
**St Paul's Cathedral School, London**

# Sunny

The sun is up in the sky looking down at us.
We sit down in the beach rubbing suncream on ourselves.
We're getting hot and sultry
There's nothing to be moody
When the sun goes down
We moan it's gone
But don't worry it will come back another day.

**Emmanuel Gbao (10)**
**Stamford Hill Primary School**

# A Baby's Summer Day

Summer is a day
A day that makes you pray for another day
Baby's all happy
Wearing just their nappy

Baby's eating ice cream
With a smile that beams
Little girls and boys
Playing with toys

So, so hot
Babies cry for their bot, bot

Babies dribble
While they giggle
At the end of the day babies laugh
While they take their bath
Babies fall off in a deep, deep sleep.

**Rebecca Irving (11)**
**Stamford Hill Primary School**

# Roller Coaster

In the gentle breeze
I get on a rollercoaster
Whoosh up and down
The wind through my hair

Round and round
The rollercoaster goes
Making me laugh
And making me sick

Rollercoaster's are so fun
They make me scream for more
When I go up I can see the world
Flash before my eyes

When I am up high
I like it
When I am down
Everything speeds past me
Like you're on a plane
Up high.

**Bianca Shaw (11)**
**Stamford Hill Primary School**

# The Fairy Chant

Chanting is golden
Chanting is good
Come with me fairies
I think you should.

Sit where the cat sits
Cross your toes
Close your eyes
And smell a rose
And say these words
Under your breath
I believe in fairies
Sure as death.

Gladflypins, Gladtrypins, Gutterpuss
And Cass come to me
Fairly each lad and lass.

If you don't
You will be scared
You won't be able to compare
It's not such a big world
After all
At least you won't have
To face the wall.

You choose the fairies
Good you're near
What did I tell you
There's nothing to fear.

**Saffron Morris  (10)**
**Stamford Hill Primary School**

# Exploring The World!

S ummer
U ganda was a treat,
M y friends and I always meet.
M y career is important and I make new mates.
E verlasting sunshine, that was great,
R emember the river glistening so.

I wish I could go back in the summer,
I wish, I wish, I wish.

A utumn
U seless dead leaves,
T earing in the cooling breeze.
U ncalled for rain,
M essing up Africa's plains.
N ever wanting to leave such a beautiful country.

I long to go back in autumn
I long, I long, I long.

W inter
I cy mountains in Peru,
N ever climbed Mount Everest, have you?
T hough I would love to ski,
E nding my pointless phone calls, no one will come with me.
R eassuring myself I will come again.

I wonder if I will go back in the winter,
I wonder, I wonder, I wonder.

S pring
P eople gardening and having fun,
R ecently there has been a lot of sun.
I stayed in England for this spring,
N ever wanted to stay but I got a bee sting.
G ets very sore and I'm allergic you see.

Maybe just maybe I will stay in England,
Maybe, maybe, just maybe.

**Tasha Shaw (11)**
**Stamford Hill Primary School**

# Season

Come, come to the summer in London, enjoy it,
Will it last?
You can go to a swimming pool and it's burning,
It's over thirty and you will get sweaty
And wear a thin layer for clothing
The sun is blazing as a colour yellow
It's hot and you will need a big bottle of water to drink.

Come, come to London to see summer
And the blue clear sky and its grey, blue and white
It looks like a whitey bluey colour
Like a blue pencil and a white pencil.

Come, come to London to see summer
And the clouds are puffy and soft also white
They also look like snow and it looks like candyfloss.

Come, come . . .

**Nathaniel Sesstein  (11)**
**Stamford Hill Primary School**

# Summer

Summer is great, summer is nice
Summer means sunshine, summer means light
Summer is hot, summer is bright,
Summer is a good time to stay out at night
Summer is sunshine through the air
Summer is a time for joy and care
Flowers are blooming there, summer is cool
So let's go to a pool
Great times to remember, this summer is cool
I like summer it makes me feel cool
Especially away from my school
These are the things I like about summer.

**Timi Ayoola (11)**
**Stamford Hill Primary School**

# School

Don't be a fool
Go to school
If you get an education
You might be able to set a formation.
Have friends at school
And you'll be cool.

Don't be late for class
And in your SATs you'll pass.

**Sedar Kinali  (11)**
**Stamford Hill Primary School**

# Love

Love if full of hope
Hope is full of kindness.
Kindness is full of wonder.
Wonder is full of love.
Love comes from motherhood.
That's why my mother had me.

**Brooke Irby  (9)**
**The Vale School**

# Dan

Dan, Dan the lavatory man
Washed his face,
In a frying pan
It went black
And he picked off the plaque.

**Isobel Powell  (9)**
**The Vale School**

# Nightmare

Tossing and turning,
Moving around,
It's like you can't escape it,
It got in your head,
You're stuck in bed,
And the ghouls are out to get you,
You're running around
Trying not to make a sound,
Being chased by werewolves,
You can't get away,
The monsters all approach you,
Then suddenly it's a brand new day.

**Anna Allgaier  (9)**
**The Vale School**

# Spring

Spring is now here,
It is an enjoyable time of the year.
When the sun is out,
And people are out and about.
Many plants and flowers are growing,
When the gardeners are mowing.
All the bright colours are coming,
And all the birds are humming.
Lots of people are lying down in the sun,
When children are having lots of fun.
Lots of people are exercising,
In many different shapes and sizes.
We all like walking down the beautiful paths,
With lovely and fresh green grass.

**Nadine Asfour (10)**
**The Vale School**

# Wonders Of Fight

In the boat, out the boat
We are so confused
Lost in the wonders of fight
I have never read a manuscript in my life
Anglo-Saxons scared and weary.
Dragonheads coming fast and scary over the deep, blue sea
The Vikings are here, the Vikings are here
People screaming and running everywhere
Attacking the monastery, killing the monks
Taking them as slaves for months and months.

**Raymond Obi  (9)**
**Turnham Primary School**

# Viking Battle Plans

'Are you ready and willing to sail to a distant land,
And win the most important battle of all?'
'I'm willing to stand up brave and tall.'
'My, oh my, you are a perfect lad.'
'Very much like my Viking dad.'

'We'll ruin this Saxons' special feast
So you've got to fight like a vicious beast
Turn over tables, break some chairs
Like I said, fight like bears
The Saxons will never, ever defeat us
Even if they try really hard to please us.

We'll kick open those doors
After that I want to hear some roars
I want to see you all with your small knives
Oh I almost forgot, are you willing to risk your lives?
I'm sure you are because you were trained by me
Now let's sail to Britain across the sea.'

**Chevelle Grey  (9)**
**Turnham Primary School**

# Viking Invasion

Did you know Vikings were born in Scandinavia?
They invaded Britain and the Anglo-Saxon churches destroyed,
Animals killed and precious things stolen.
The Anglo-Saxons would fight them
They would never give up
But thousands got killed and injured
They cried and cried until they lost the war.

**Aïchetou Nanfon (9)**
**Turnham Primary School**

# Anglo-Saxons

Anglo-Saxons always battle
And all the parents don't like it at all.
Children just want to eat a meal
And Anglo-Saxons just want to kill.
When the Vikings came they all went mad
And all the children they went sad.

**Jessica Brisibe (9)**
**Turnham Primary School**

# Vikings

The Vikings are tough and strong but they did pong.
They invaded Britain and killed men.
They stole people's money to pay their bills
They came in their boats.
They were very long.
They killed the monks and destroyed the monasteries.
It all happened in 871AD.

**Luke Tan  (9)**
**Turnham Primary School**

# The Vikings

The Vikings were a tribe
Who plundered everyone
They even killed the monks
And said their job was done

The Vikings were beasts
At the end of the day
They had all their feasts
At the end of the day

The Vikings owned ships
With painted dragon faces
The boat was curved
For all their money cases

The Vikings were people
Who were very, very bad
The monks were tired
And said the Vikings were mad

The monks were killed
For all their beliefs
The Vikings didn't care
Unless their treasures were received.

**Imahra Skelly-Gill  (9)**
**Turnham Primary School**

# Anglo-Vikes

Many, many years ago,
There was a tribe of Vikings
They invaded Britain like crashes of lightning.

Then we have the Anglo-Saxons
They weren't so bad,
But when they saw the Vikings coming
That's when they went mad.

The Vikings grabbed their swords and shields
And charged down the hills,
Some went into people's houses and
Took the money for their bills.

But the point I'm trying to make
Is not a piece of cake.

What I'm trying hard to say,
Is that the Vikings invaded Britain
In the nastiest possible way!

**Malikah James (9)**
**Turnham Primary School**

# The Vikings

Many years ago from now,
There were Vikings and Anglo-Saxons.
In battle they had swords, shields and helmets.
The Vikings have a powerful god,
Called Thor and when they die they go to their Valhalla.
The Vikings raided Lindisfarne and
Destroyed the monasteries.
They killed the monks and stole the gold,
And took some monks as slaves.
Then the Vikings invaded Britain and
Killed the Anglo-Saxons but they weren't very brave.

**Deborah Dike  (9)**
**Turnham Primary School**

# Troy And The Wooden Horse

Wooden horse carved by Epious
'Oh Paris why did you take my wife?
Oh in the end I will get her back.'
Down to Troy in their horse
Emperors came crowding around
'No, get out of my way'
'How did they make this?' people shouted
'Oh look, look I can see Troy and its Trojans'
'Ready men, yes!'
Slowly one by one people got killed
Everyone died, the whole of Troy.

**Charlie Ward  (8)**
**Turnham Primary School**

# Trojans' War

People killing here and there
Trojans fighting everywhere.
Woman screaming, children crying
Soldiers injured, soldiers dying.
Trojans sleeping, Trojans death,
All the Greeks are out of breath.
Ancient Greeks are all dying
And all the Trojans are crying.
Paris met with Helen all this time
Paris calls 'Now she's mine!'
Ancient Greeks hide in the horse,
Now you will have to force.
All the Greeks killed Trojans with their sword,
They came from the wooden horse's door.

**Puja Luthra  (8)**
**Turnham Primary School**

# The Troy

People killing here and there
Trojans fighting everywhere
Women screaming, children crying
Soldiers injured soldiers dying
Warriors leaving people with blood so close
Shields blocking swords
Swords getting used to kill
Battle everywhere.

**Akyrie Palmer  (8)**
**Turnham Primary School**

# The War About Greece And The Trojans

People killing here and there
Trojans fighting everywhere
Women screaming, children crying
Soldiers injured, soldiers dying
Greek people are making Trojans run
Trojans said 'This ain't fun'
Trojans are lying dead and still
Trojans' skins begins to chill
All the Greeks climb up the hill
Trojans think that they could kill
Now it is time to go home
Now we are going across to roam.

**Charlene Williams (8)**
**Turnham Primary School**

# The Trojan War

People killing here and there
Trojans fighting everywhere
Women fighting, children crying
Soldiers injured, soldiers dying
People dying from generation to generation
How do people get through rations?
Greek people saying let's get bombs
Children saying it's not fun
People on horses
Pushing their forces
People injured, children dying
People won't prove they're lying
All people running up hills
People saying they're going to kill.

**Rhea Carter (8)**
**Turnham Primary School**

# The History War Poem

People killing here and there
Trojans fighting everywhere.
Women screaming, children crying,
Soldiers injured, soldiers dying.
Sounds of explosions
War of Trojans.
Sign of sad news
Terrifying bad news!
All the Greeks dying of sorrow
All the soldiers throwing spears and arrows.
Smell of victory
Sadness history.
Bad imaginations.
Frightening concentrations.

**Armena Arumaithurai (8)**
**Turnham Primary School**

# The Letter Of Achilles

To Menelaus
As he sailed to Troy
We shouted 'Victory is ours!'
We saw the wooden horse
Ashore we went up ahead, we saw
Sinon's torch up high, we said
'It was time for Troy to die'
We came into the city square
Women, children crying everywhere
As I pierced Paris's heart when
He was just about to wake
We have taken Helen back now
We are sailing back from Achilles.

**Isaac Fatukasi  (8)**
**Turnham Primary School**

# Early March

The cock is crowing,
The stream is flowing.
The small birds twitter,
The lake does glitter.
The green field sleeps in the sun,
The oldest and the youngest,
At work with the strongest,
The cattle are grazing their heads never raising.
There are forty feeding as one,
Like an army defeated,
The snow has retreated
And now doth fare ill
On top of the bare hill.
Small clouds are sailing, blue sky retrieving,
The rain is over and gone.

**Tré Barrett  (8)**
**Turnham Primary School**

# Ten Year Fight

There was a boy called Troy who sat on a sharp toy.
There was a boy from Spain who sat on a drain.
There was a man from Paris who called himself Harris.
There was a boy called Troy who sat on a little boy.
There was a boy from Troy who played with his toys.
There was a girl from Troy who spat on a toy.

**Draven Foster  (7)**
**Turnham Primary School**

# The Trojan War Poem

Paris was handsome,
At least he thought he was.
When he sailed across the sea,
He saw Helen and said 'That girl's for me.'
Paris was a naughty boy,
So he kidnapped Helen and took her away.
When he got back he saw some ships,
That looked like a flick.
The king said 'You are stupid, look what you have done,
And I need to get my gun.'
The Trojan War lasted for a long time,
It was not fun at all.
The war lasted for a whole ten years.

**Andrew Owusu-Aninakwah  (7)**
**Turnham Primary School**

# Trojan Poem

Once upon a time in the land of Troy
There was a naughty boy.
Paris went to Sparta to swap places but instead took Helen,
King Menelaus said Paris committed a felon.
Troy and Sparta went to a battlefield,
They all had a shield.
Paris started this war that was very boring,
Paris thought Troy was hammering him.
Achilles killed Hector from Sparta,
'Trojans you should've been smarter!'
Sparta made secret plans and killed the Trojans, the silly boys.

**Joshua Holder  (8)**
**Turnham Primary School**

# The Trojan War

There once was a prince called Paris.
He was blessed by Aphrodite to win Queen Helen
So he went on a boat to get Queen Helen
As long as he was away King Menelaus woke up
So King Menelaus went and told his guards
That someone had kidnapped Queen Helen
And Odysseus had a plan, he said,
'We should build a wooden horse.'

**Pierre Armani (8)**
**Turnham Primary School**

# My Name Is Hannah

H is the name I never knew,
A hhh I know why you're amused.
N aana, you can't catch me,
N o not there, can't you see?
A big fat cat,
H id under the mat.

J JB sports,
O h no, where are the shorts?
H annah, your name is high,
N o, not the blue sky.

**Hannah John  (8)**
**Turnham Primary School**

# An Argument

'No I won't'
'If you don't'
'I told you, I won't!'
'You will!
Stay still'
'That's going to hurt.'
'Get in your skirts'
'Do I have to?
I hate having to wear a tutu'
'Put on your ballet shoe'
'Cooey'
'Here she is,
With a bottle of fizz,
To celebrate you getting a part in the Wiz'
'Cooey'
'Go let her in'
'Don't go making a din'
'Don't make me commit a sin'
'Go and let her in'
'Orangeade is what I've got'
'Oh you got an awful lot'
'I don't know how we'll drink it all'
'You may take some to school'
'Wow! Mum! Wicked! Cool!'

**Amy Steer  (10)**
**Turnham Primary School**

# My Poem

This boy called Jake,
Ate a snake,
Down by the river lake,
My best friend Jake,
Had a big backpack,
It was all in black,
He told me it was heavy for his back,
'Slow down mate,
I've just ate,'
'But Kate,
You're late.'
I went in the gate,
Today's the 1st of May,
I'm going shopping today,
At school we play with clay,
No, come this way,
I saw a van,
With a giant man,
In the back was a rock star band,
The rock band was very great,
So I decided to go and see them with my mate,
We went over and said 'Hi'
They were rude and said 'Bye-bye'
So we walked away,
Then they shouted out and said
'I hope you're coming to see us in May.'

**Romaine McLean  (11)**
**Turnham Primary School**

# The Best

Madrid are better than the rest
So come we're buying George Best
We're having a little feast and
Guess what, we're having a surprise
Guest which is George Best
We're in a bit of a mess
We are low on money
It's kind of funny it
Was all because of a
Cute little bunny
We though we had money
But wait until you see this bunny
It sells lots of honey
And receives lots of money.

**Marlon Bowen  (11)**
**Turnham Primary School**

# Viking

A Viking is a king that
Doesn't do a thing.
A boat that floats that swims through the water.
A goat that jokes that makes you laugh.
My muscles are aching
I must be fainting.
I'm being haunted
I must be exhausted
On this Viking long ship.
I'm so furious I could
Strangle your neck.
If I die help me come alive again
No way
Don't you know Vikings are
Evil.

**Rashidat Giwa (9)**
**Turnham Primary School**

# Destruction

A deadly roar
A terrifying fright
A god of war working all night

A herd of bulls
A piece of tool
A torturing school

A heard of thunder
A sight of lightning
Everything is just frightening
A cut of your leg
And an everlasting eruption
This is called *destruction.*

**Jordan Asare-Gyimah  (8)**
**Turnham Primary School**

# In The Sky

There I was in the sky,
Dreaming of apple pie.

Then there were some Vikings,
The lead one was wearing rings.

Then they came on the shore,
Rowing with their long, long oars.

Then they jumped out to fight,
Using up all their might.

They fought Saxons more and more,
Then the Saxons said, 'You score.'

But no, they fought and made them fight all night,
All the Saxons wanted to do was snuggle up tight.

They had to plead, they couldn't
All they could do was be dead

So there I was in the sky,
Just witnessing people die.

My clock was ticking, tick-tock,
Oh look its 9 o'clock.

Now look I'm a sleepy head,
So I'll say it's time for bed.

Goodnight.

**Isabel Brown  (9)**
**Turnham Primary School**

# The Vikings Ride

Vikings brave
Vikings afraid
Rowing in their long boats.
With fifty folks rowing a boat.
Viking boats ninety feet long and fifty feet wide.
When Vikings ride the tide.
Vikings ride up and down in the stormy night.
Vikings fight every night.
But you'd better beware because you might have a nasty fright.
Think of their kids and wife.
Thinking, *will I survive?*
*Will I meet my own death?*
Vikings pushing the oars rowing forwards and backwards
Their muscles shining with sweat.
When Vikings have war they move through mist, smoke and thunder
Striking the houses showing a sign they are coming.
Hiding in caves waiting to scare and tear their heads off.

**River Foster**
**Turnham Primary School**

# A Viking Fight

Stamp, stamp, stamp running through the park
Along came a man who said, 'Bark, bark'
Now one day I saw a Viking man
Along came a man and ran
Viking warrior sailing across the night
Along comes a man and calls for a fight
So this man came to my house
But when I saw him probably he was a mouse
So he ran and ran
And he sang
Running, running through the day
He runs and runs and starts May.

**Ibraahiim Mohamed**
**Turnham Primary School**

# The Big Fight

I went on holiday to see Vikings on the bay,
But when I got there I wanted to stay.
Then the Vikings charged
And the Anglo-Saxons barged.
Then they ended up into a fight
Until it was right.
When they stopped they had supper
But there was no butter.
They drank out of horns
And somebody fell in thorns.
Then it was midnight and
The Vikings said 'Bye'
And the Anglo-Saxons sigh
But they had a lot of pie.

**Chuck Henriques  (8)**
**Turnham Primary School**

# The Anglo-Saxons

The Anglo-Saxons invaded Britain.
They came and litter Britain.
They came and they were fighting.
They came and shouted louder than lightning.
They robbed the houses.
They stole and killed.
They came with their shields.
They came across fields.
They ran and ran.
As fast as they can.
This is the end of my poem
Once upon the time this happened.

**Natasha Stanic-Stewart  (9)**
**Turnham Primary School**

# The Ten Years Of The Trojan War

People killing here and there,
Trojans fighting everywhere
Women screaming, children crying,
Soldiers injured, soldiers dying,
Seeing blood, seeing death,
Seeing soldiers taking breath,
Nightmares about spears and blood,
And seeing all the houses flood,
Greeks will kill,
And give their will
Children moan and moan,
Because Queen Helen is put back on her throne.

**Camila Arias  (8)**
**Turnham Primary School**

# Trojan War Poem

People killing here and there
Trojans fighting everywhere
Women screaming, children crying,
Soldiers injured, solders dying
Seeing soldiers, seeing death
Seeing soldiers taking a breath
The Greeks build the wooden horse
On Odysseus' command and used their force.

**Nicole Tang (8)**
**Turnham Primary School**

# Trojans' War Poem

T roy will be destroyed
R ound shield ready for battle
O ver the water the boats skim
J ustice for Paris's wife
A gamemnon found Helen
N ow we must go home

W ar with Greeks and Troy
A chilles is the strongest warrior
R eady to kill.

**Jordan Swaby  (8)**
**Turnham Primary School**

# War Of Troy

Achilles killing everybody who faces him.
Across the water Greeks' boats skim.
Trojans trying to kill the Greeks.
But the Trojans have to stop and eat.
The Greeks beat the Trojans and capture Helen.
After the Greeks ate a melon.

**Oliver Hughes  (8)**
**Turnham Primary School**

# Back To Sparta

Warriors killing here and there.
Trojans fighting everywhere.

Women screaming, children crying.
Warriors wounded, soldiers dying.

Paris is trying to take Helen back to Troy
Agamemnon says 'No chance boy!'

They lived happily ever after
No more Troy but a lot of laughter.

**Jaynésha Rowe  (8)**
**Turnham Primary School**

# The Greek And Trojan War

People killing here and there
Soldiers are running everywhere
The Greeks and Trojans have a fight
They have it every night
Women screaming, children crying
Soldiers injured, soldiers dying
The Greeks will win
And everybody will grin
People are running around
Corpses lie upon the ground.

**Channin Jackson  (8)**
**Turnham Primary School**

# Troy And The Wooden Horse

People kill here and there
Trojans fighting everywhere
Women screaming, children crying
Soldiers injured, soldiers dying
Blood running down peoples' chests
Greeks shouting 'We're the best'
Epious built a wooden horse
Thirty men hid within a horse
Thirty men came out at night
And the Trojans lost the fight.

**Taylor-Jay Heward  (8)**
**Turnham Primary School**

# My Story Of The Trojan War

People killing here and there
Trojans fighting everywhere
Women screaming, children crying
Soldiers injured, soldiers dying
I can hear the sound of sorrow
I wonder if I'm here tomorrow?
I can taste the blood of children
How does it feel fighting?
It's just like a spark of lightning.
Please help me Almighty One
Don't let people kill me.
Because I just don't want
To die yet till my job is done.

**Ndey Cham  (8)**
**Turnham Primary School**

# Best Friends

You know I'm here all the way,
I miss your voice every single day.
I wish my mum and dad didn't catch us running away,
It will be our first birthday apart in May.

I'm not speaking to my mum,
She wouldn't let me eat your bun.
My granddad is great to talk to,
I really could talk more to you.

It was good to remember the times we had,
It made me happy and glad.
Biscuits shouldn't have opened his big trap,
We would have been in London picking our lovely mat.

I know you live in Scotland,
And I know it's so far away.
But you can visit me in England,
And we can start day by day.

You are my number one best friend,
I will never let that end.
I guess this is goodbye but not forever,
I have to go, my mum is feeling under the weather.

**Winnie Inneh (10)**
**Turnham Primary School**

# My Family

My family are described in many ways,
If I told you all of them it would take me days.

Some of them can be funny, sad and nasty,
Some of them can even be classy.

My family and I love going to places,
We like seeing familiar faces.

I like seeing my family smile,
Even if it's for a little while.

If I had to go away,
I'd miss them every single day.

I love my family lots and lots,
I thank them for everything I've got.

I simply want to say to all of you,
I love you, I love you, and I love you.

Friends are special friends are great,
Anyone who's our friend is our best mate.
My family can be funny,
I love going shopping with my mummy.
Lovely people my family can be,
You know they light my face with glee.
They're my family, I love them dearly,
Can't you see they're lovely, clearly?

**Chloe Derby  (10)**
**Turnham Primary School**

# My Annoying Little Brother

My annoying little brother
I would swap him for another.

You'd recognise him in a crowd
He'll be the one roaring loud.

When he's in trouble he's really bad
But everyone knows he's just mad.

All the time, everyday he is rude
And at times he is stupid and crude.

When he doesn't eat his dinner
He gets thinner and thinner.

To our mum he isn't helpful
But at times he is cool.

My little bro is extremely lazy
I'd describe with the word . . . crazy.

My brother is a sad, sad soul
I wish he was a nice little boy who played with a doll.

I love him, I love him, I really do
Hopefully he knows it's true.

He's my annoying little brother,
I wouldn't swap him for another.

**Rachel Ackred (10)**
**Turnham Primary School**

# My Best Friend

My best friend is a dancer
She loves to sing
She wears bling, bling,
She shakes her bum
But does not like to be rude
To her mum,
She once had a fever
But she's still quite a diva.

**Sinea Ramgoolam  (11)**
**Turnham Primary School**

# Summer

S ummer is hot and very dry
U sually and seriously it's not a lie
M argate beach we always go
M e and my family perform a show
E veryone's having fun all through the day
R est tonight then go on holiday.

**Michael Solarin (11)**
**Turnham Primary School**

# Seasons Coming

Summer brings the hot sun in our lives,
Cutting fresh fruits with very sharp knives.
Swimming around in the deep blue sea,
Running from the insects especially the bees.

Winter is a season that I really enjoy,
Presents for everyone like teddy bears and toys.
Christmas time it's coming, it's very, very near,
But my brother gets more presents, that hardly seems fair.

Autumn is excitement that occurs all around,
Hearing people singing a very loud sound.
You can hear the fireworks with a big bang,
Dress up like Dracula and his very sharp fangs.

Spring is a season that everyone enjoys,
Buying lots of chocolates for little girls and boys.
Springtime is a season that I spend outside
Going on the rollercoaster and other special rides.

**Niche Gillespie (11)**
**Turnham Primary School**

# My Favourite Things . . .

My favourite things . . .
My little sister plays with my hair and when
I tell her to stop she doesn't care.

On paper my little brother likes to write
But with me he likes to fight.

My knickers are navy blue
And very comfortable and
I don't want to wear any other shoe.

My CDs make me want to dance
My mother plays Bee Gees at least they give me a chance.

My best friend is honest and caring
She's always thinking nice of me.
She's very kind and very daring
And that's how it should be.

That's the end of the story about my best friend,
My mother is very nice, she smiles and when we go out
She buys me things she doesn't care the price
And she doesn't want me to be wild
And I did save the best to the last.

**Thelma Ajudua  (11)**
**Turnham Primary School**

# Family And Friends

My dog Misty is always the best,
Zac told me he had a cloud on his chest.
Ronnie is super funny,
My sister is as nice as a bunny.
My mum is the greatest,
Tommy has all the latest.
I think Niche is the best at chess,
My niece and nephews make a mess.
Michael is scared of a spider,
My brother David looks like Strider.
Darryl is never late,
And he beats me when we skate.

**Adam Cook (11)**
**Turnham Primary School**

# Summer

Summer makes me happy,
It makes me play all day.
I love to eat my ice cream,
And go on holiday.

Swimming in my swimming pool,
Sunbathing on the beach.
I love to do all these things,
And eating fruits like peach.

Having a barbecue on the beach,
Eating chicken kebabs.
Watching the sunset go down,
Ignoring all the crabs.

**Kirstie O'Connell (11)**
**Turnham Primary School**

# My Four Best Friends

M y best friends are really funny
Y ou know they make me feel like honey

F or when they are not near me
O f course I feel glum
U rgently in need of help it comes quickly
R eady for a challenge it will come quite rarely

B onita is the writer of this poem
E verytime I'm upset I start weeping
S taring at the magazine page
T elling me about being engaged

F rom all the happy times we had
R embering those things that made me glad
I t takes a lot of guts to become a friend
E verytime I'm with them I know that our friendship will never end
N ever ruin happy thoughts
D elighting all the secrets shared
S haring the truth and double dares.

**Bonita Pryce-Green  (11)**
**Turnham Primary School**

# Summer

Summer weather is the best
The heat you feel underneath your vest
Butterflies, fluttering in the blue sky
Summer is a good season, that's no lie
People chilling out in the parks
I can hear singing from a singing lark
Everyone's happy at this time of the year
There's no need to worry! Have no fear!
Well this season is summer, hip, hip hooray!
Now it's time to chill out on this sunny day!

**Akilah Bomani  (11)**
**Turnham Primary School**

# Winters

W inter's cold and chilly snow!
  I cy winds have got to go!
N ecks, ears and toes are ice!
T ogether playing with snow is nice!
E ver had frostbite?
R eady for a snowball fight!
S ometimes the feeling is right!

**Marion Brown (11)**
**Turnham Primary School**

# Summer

S ummer is fun I'd love to jump in the sun.
U nder the water I see my aunt's daughter.
M y mum and I go to Florida.
M y friends and I tell a lie.
E veryday I go we laugh and play.
R oses I smell, they smell like perfume.

**Sharell McDonald  (11)**
**Turnham Primary School**

# Winter

Winter is the day when everyone has fun
Willing to get out and have a bit of a run.

Icy and cold when winter comes
My dad always has a bit of rum.

Never eat outside
And always ask to have a bicycle ride.

I asked my mum and dad to buy me warm clothes
And have a bit of toast.

**Satheesan Sriskantharajah  (11)**
**Turnham Primary School**

# My Aunt Annabella's Abnormal Apple Pie!

My aunt Annabella
Is unusually clever
Her food, I'm afraid
Is not quite the same

When in the warm kitchen
She pulls out her mittens
And adds to the mix
A terrible fix

In the pie there are . . .
Dirty nails
Fragile, but frail
Slippery snails
Oxen's tails

My Aunt she serves it up in a dish
Accompanied with roasted fish.
I take a breath and close my eyes
As if I'm just about to die

I opened my mouth to take a bite
The taste gave me an awful fright
I spat everything out, bit by bit
To show I didn't enjoy it

The word pie makes me sick
It makes my saliva run really thick!
I'll never taste a pie for my life
No matter how much I struggle and strife!

**Olivia Ogolo (11)**
**Turnham Primary School**

# Vikings Are Coming

'Vikings are coming
So stop your humming
*And run!*

They're going to invade our green land
And turn us into stiff sand

They'll come in the dark night
So get prepared for a long fight

Do you now see?
*Oh no, they got me!'*

**EJ Hall  (9)**
**Turnham Primary School**

# The Vikings

Long ago Viking warriors rode across the blue, cold ocean
In their long, wooden boats.
Pushing and pulling their oars all day long.
Viking arms work and were aching.
Muscles exhausted like running legs.
Viking warriors lived long ago in little houses.
They rode through the blue, cold sea to Britain
To steal gold and silver and green land.
They came out of their long boats
Standing big and blonde.
We take all the land, burn down their property
And make our own house
Stealing was their lives.

**Ruby Crowley  (9)**
**Turnham Primary School**

# Viking

Rowing and rowing through the night
Long ship rower sits up tight
To keep the cold away.

Eating food in the night
How do you survive?

Keep on going, keep on going
You will stay alive.

They came in the night
And took all the goods
And went back in the morning,
Shh! Keep quiet.

**Sharlene Roach**
**Turnham Primary School**

# My PlayStation 2

I like to play on my PlayStation 2,
My hands stick to the controls like glue,
I really like playing my wrestling game,
Because that one puts all the others to shame!
I play on it every night and day,
And if I play anymore I'll start going insane,
I'll keep it and play on it forever and ever,
And I'll never stop playing it never, ever.

**Alfie Andrews-Smith  (11)**
**Turnham Primary School**

# Vikings Invade

This is set twelve hundred years ago
The Vikings came and attacked, *Wow!*
Monasteries are gone, the monks live no longer.

Battleaxes, dragon heads
Monks bringing people to hospital beds.
Clang, clash the swords fight,
Look there's more on my right.

The sounds go lower and lower
The Viking row and row
Bye-bye Anglo-Saxons
We will never see you again.

**Orianne Lunguma Afikwel (9)**
**Turnham Primary School**

# Football

A rsene Wenger is the best coach
R onaldo at Man United plays like a cockroach
S illy Pires slapping opponent's faces
E ver never losing places
N ever losing
A lways cruising
L egs are moving.

F eet are moving,
O ver the goal, offside, no goal or point
O riginal T-shirts are not allowed for the team
T hiery Henry plays for the best screamers
B alls are flying up in the air
A udience always jumps and cheers
L egs are floating
L egs are fouling.

**Aniefiok Umo  (7)**
**Turnham Primary School**

# The Trojan War

Paris was Prince of Troy
He was a very naughty boy,
Aphrodite rewarded Paris by marrying Helen
When Paris saw Helen
He thought she was as juicy as a melon
When Paris stole Helen,
He committed a serious felon
When the Trojan War begun,
It was not at all fun.

**Sekani Trotman  (7)**
**Turnham Primary School**

# The French Football Team

The French team is the best,
Better than England,
And the rest.

Thierry Henry is running past everyone,
No one can stop him
The best defenders will come,
But they are dumb.

One goal to add to their collection
There they go,
In the goalkeeper's section.

The final whistle blows,
They win the trophy,
There it goes.

**Robert O'Shea (11)**
**Turnham Primary School**

# Nature

In a river the water flows
In the sky the wind blows,
In the earth worms dig
To protect themselves from the big.

In the woods there are chopped down trees
Now there's not a lot of breeze.
There is a lot of grass
But what spoils it is the glass.

Plants love the sun and rain
Plants don't live on the plain
Plants live in the soil
And they are not wrapped in foil.

Some trees grow grapes
But no trees grow tapes.
Apples grow on trees
While honey is made by bees.

**Haran Thevaratnam  (10)**
**Turnham Primary School**

# I Love Being Me!

Able to see,
Able to walk,
Able to touch,
Able to talk,
I love being me!

Able to write,
Able to think,
Able to sleep,
Able to link,
I love being me!

I like the teachers,
They like me,
I like the pupils,
They come to my house for tea,
I love being me!

**Keishelle Charles (11)**
**Turnham Primary School**

# Under The Sea

Wearing my diving kit,
Admiring the ocean sea,
Brave enough to go down there,
There's no one here but me.

All is quiet, all is calm,
Surrounded by exotic fish,
Swimming in the salty waters,
No noise, like your teacher's wish!

Clown fish, sea horses,
A flying fish too!
I looked at it with fascination,
After a while, away it flew!

Amazing dolphins striding swiftly,
Two minutes left until I'm out of breath,
Should I leave
Or should I wait for death?

**Dzung Doan  (11)**
**Turnham Primary School**

# The World Cup

Lots of men kicking a ball,
It looks like a draw, yes two all!

Scoring goals is what they do,
If they lose we all shout 'Boo-hoo!'

Oh no, someone's been given the yellow card
They pushed someone, they should be barred.

Thanks to Beckham's best kick,
We got into the championships!

Sven is pleased about the news,
He thinks that we deserve a cruise.

We have won the World Cup,
We're all crying, ah cheer up!

**Lara Elson (11)**
**Turnham Primary School**

# The Rolling Meatball

I was eating spaghetti
It tasted just great,
When one of the meatballs
Jumped off my plate.

Before I could ask
My mother for more,
It rolled in the kitchen
And out through the door.

I tried to catch it
But I tried in vain,
It rolled down the road
And fell down a drain.

I rang the police
And the fire brigade,
Who arrived with a net
A rope and a spade.

They scooped it out
It was covered in slime
'Thank you' I cried
And without waiting time.

Hurried back home
Where the meatball, of course,
I ate in a dollop
Of tomato sauce.

**Rhian Williams (11)**
**Turnham Primary School**